In Loving Memory

Poetry on the Loss of a Child

June E. Shelly

3rd edition

This book is dedicated
to all parents
who have lost a child,
in loving memory
of all those children.

Contents

1 In the Beginning   7

   Scripture - Psalm 139:13-14   8

   Letter of sympathy   9

   Our Love for James   10

   Mother to Son   12

   Feelings   13

   Scripture - Matthew 2:18   14

2 Death   15

   In the Incubator - illustration   16

   Denial   17

   Too Young   18

   My Son is Dead   19

   Yesterday, Today, Tomorrow   20

   The Hurt, The Strength   21

   Tomorrow Will Come   21

   Scripture - Matthew 19:13-14   22

3 Remembering   23

   Mother and Child - illustration   24

   Remembering   25

   Why Me?   26

   The Worst Day   27

   I Am a Mother   28

The Difference 29

Sometimes It's Not Enough 29

Scripture - Psalm 23 30

4 Grieving 31

Child Angel - illustration 32

Carry Me, Jesus 33

Grief 34

Let Me Feel 35

Who Are We Unshared? 36

I Depend on You 37

Scripture - 2 Corinthians 1:3-4 38

5 Living 39

A Loving Touch - illustration 40

We Are in This Together 41

Guilt 42

God Grant Me 43

Believing 44

Thanks 45

Scripture - Revelation 21:1-6 46

Index 47

In the Beginning

For thou didst form my inward parts:
Thou didst cover me in my mother's womb.
I will give thanks unto thee;
for I am fearfully and wonderfully made:
Wonderful are thy works;
And that my soul knoweth right well.

Psalm 139:13-14

September 25, 1982

Our son, James Thomas Shelly, was born on July 18, 1982, weighing 820 grams. I had carried him for 30 weeks but due to severe toxemia, a Caesarean section was done. Three days later, on July 21, 1982, he died.

A part of us died with him and to fill the void he'd left, I turned to sketching and writing poetry. Though I have often been discouraged and frustrated by my abilities, I know the attempt helped me. This book was the result, in the hope that reading it will help someone as much as writing it helped me.

It has our pain in it, our hope and joy, but mostly our love. To lose that precious bond between parent and child is heartbreaking. I hope that something of what I have written, said, or done can ease that pain or help someone else understand it.

That hope is my monument to our son. He could ask for nothing better. We could not love him in a better way.

With love and sympathy,
June and Albin Shelly

Our Love for James

In the beginning there was the seed
Born of a love shared in joy;
A first whisper of hope barely daring
To dream of a life yet to be.
At last, confirmation, a life was beginning.
We began choosing names, for a girl or a boy?
Worries and fears, hopes and dreams unending;
New thoughts and great love for the person in me.

Sharing and planning, hopes for tomorrow,
Our family rejoicing in the life just begun.
Singing you songs, telling you of love,
Listening to your heartbeat, knowing you live.
The first of your movements
soon growing stronger;
Your father feeling you,
his daughter or son.
Sharing our hopes for your future endeavours,
The growth of our love
and the new love to give.

Then unforeseen, problems arrived
And a wee baby boy met the world too soon.
Great awe, greater love, undemanding and sweet;
The treasure of loving you in your innocent charms.
New hopes and new love,
                    prayers shared with Jesus.
Your baptism given on your second afternoon.
Tears shared in friendship,
                    blue puppies from Auntie
Then life released you to sleep in Jesus' arms.

Wrapped in blue blanket
                    your grandmother gave you
With flowers from your family
                    on your casket so small;
Commended to the soil and your spirit in heaven,
The final leave-taking, the replacing of sod.
The Lord is our shepherd, he leads us with love
Though the pattern of his methods
                    may puzzle us all.
We rejoice in the life we were blessed to be given;
The child whom we treasured
                    till your return to God.

Our memories will comfort, you live in our love,
Our flower ever blooming in the heavens above.

Mother to Son

I gave you the life you held so briefly,
So preciously.
I touched your tiny hands -
You tried to hold my finger,
Too big for your palm.
I loved you. I ache with that love,
An ache of joy and pain,
Of life and death.
You gave me everything of importance -
A bonding so sweet and strong
That it will hold me till the end of my days
    And beyond.
        Through every moment I hold
            You will never be forgotten
                But will live forever in the heart
                    Of I who cherished you
                        From the moment of your conception
                        In my womb
                            Beneath the heart
                                That will nurture you forever
                                    As the womb nurtured you
                                        Before your birth.

When I was pregnant, I was afraid;
Afraid I would be a poor mother,
Afraid I could not love enough,
Afraid I had too little to give.

Then I gave birth and I saw my son.
I gave him everything I had.
I gave him all the love in the world
And together we were perfect.

But then I was still afraid;
Afraid that he was too small,
Afraid that he would die,
And he did.

And now I feel everything and nothing.
I am empty and that empty aches.
I hurt and that hurt is a knife in my heart.
I love and he is not here.

Together we were everything good and right.
Together we were love and joy.
Apart, there is no we.
There is only I
And I don't know who I am
Now that I'm without him.

A voice was heard in Ramah,
Weeping and great mourning,
Rachel weeping for her children;
And she would not be comforted,
because they are not.

Matthew 2:18

Death

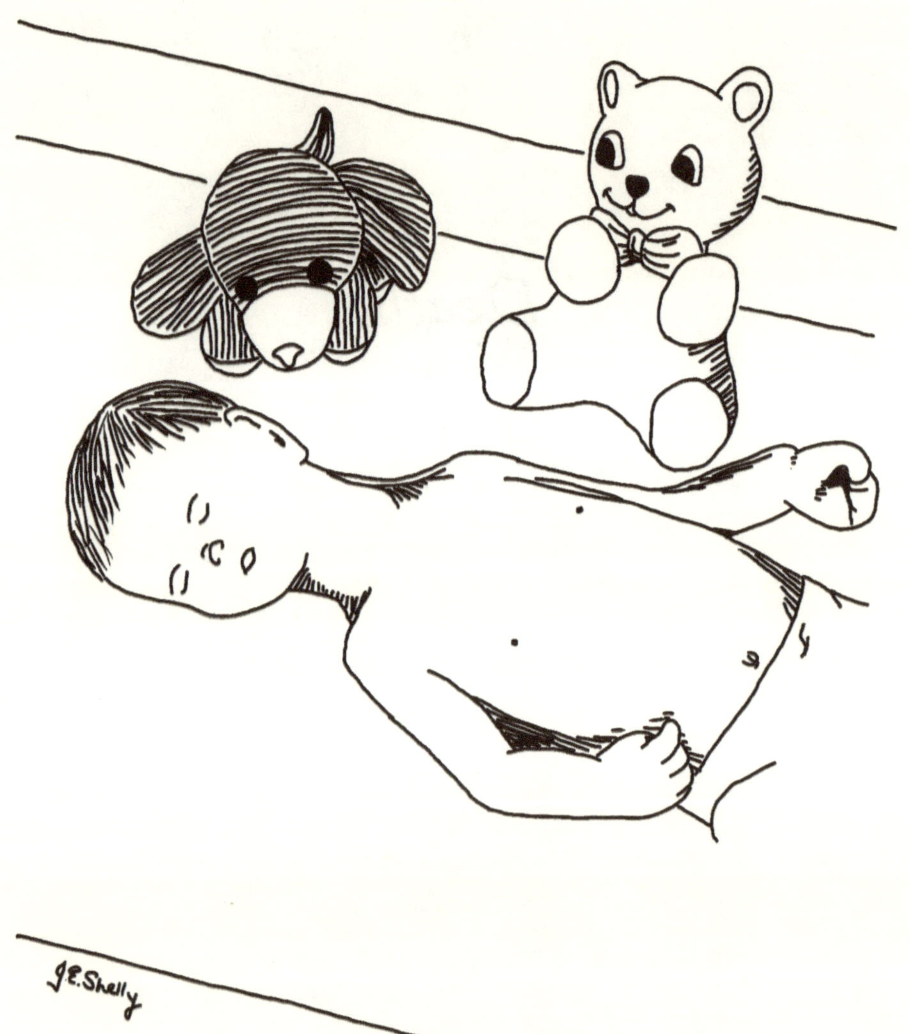

Denial

I know you are not there where last I saw you
But I am here with your memory and without you.
I deny your funeral and your casket and your grave.
If only I moved right, I could walk in and find you.
I could touch you and see you and feel you
If only I were to return.
So why don't I return?
Because I know you will not be there
And I'll lose you all over again.

Too Young

It is said that some
   Are too young, too sweet,
      Too innocent
         to live

Because in order to survive
   We must grow old, be bitter
      With knowledge
         or die.

My child was too small,
   Too premature.
      He didn't have time to grow old,
         To learn, to be strong,
            to live.

Why couldn't there be a rule
that instead of being
too young to live,
He could have been
too young
to die?

My son is dead.
Dead ...
Is such a cruel word,
Harsh, unforgiving,
Outrageous.
There are softer ways to say it -
    Passed away,
    Passed on,
    Gone,
    Asleep eternally,
    In heaven.
Only I'm still left in hell
In spite of the euphemisms.
    Death ...
    Is a cruel thing,
    Harsh, unforgiving,
    Outrageous.
There is no other way to say it
Because
    My son is dead.

Yesterday, Today, Tomorrow

Yesterday there was a pregnancy.
There were hopes and fears.
There was a birth.

Today there is a knowledge,
A separation, a death.
There is a hell.

Tomorrow is still a promise
   Without guarantees, with dreams,
      Perhaps a heaven.

      If only I can survive the hell of today,
       Then I can dream of tomorrow.

The Hurt, the Strength

When I imagined the worst that could happen,
I didn't know it would hurt this much
When it came.

When I thought how devastated
        and incapable I would be,
I didn't know how much strength I would have
For when I needed it.

Tomorrow Will Come

I believe that tomorrow will come;
If not in this dimension,
Then in the next.

For that reason, I refuse to give up,
For nothing is absolutely forsaken
If only tomorrow will come.

Then were there brought unto him little children,
that he should lay his hands on them, and pray:
and the disciples rebuked them.
But Jesus said, Suffer the little children,
and forbid them not, to come unto me:
for to such belongeth the kingdom of heaven.

Matthew 19:13-14

Remembering

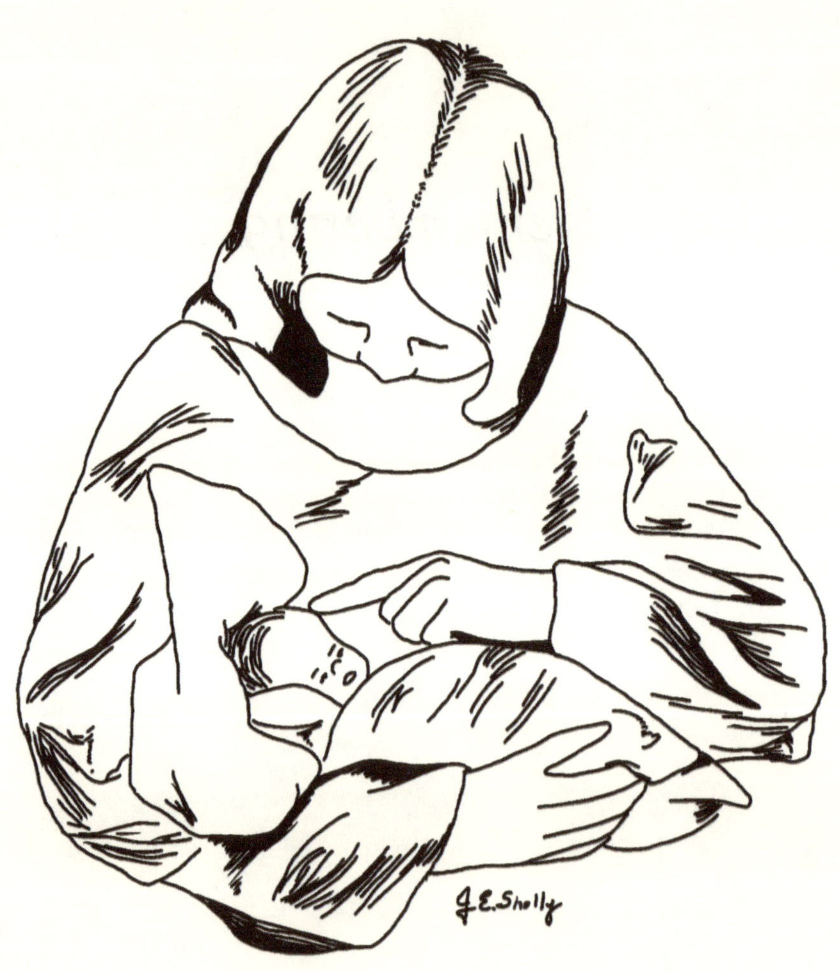

We have so few pictures of you;
I had seen you so few times.
As the days passed, I panicked to realize
I could not remember the pertness of your nose,
The contour of your cheeks,
The delicate tracing of your lips,
The gentle shape of your eyes.
Through days of frantically grasping at scraps of memory,
Carefully sketching each detail,
I drew your picture.

My friend told me to remember you,
But not to dwell;
To gaze at your picture
But not too often.
I cannot not remember,
For your absence is as tangible and real
As your presence.
I no longer desperately gaze at your picture
Trying to remember your features,
For your face is engraved on my vision.
I see you without my eyes,
I feel you with my soul.
How can I not dwell on you
When I see you and feel you in the essence of my existence?

And why would I choose to forget?
I would rather have a sorrow with your picture in it,
Than the hellish pain without you.

Why Me?

I scream out, "Why?
Why me to feel sorrow and pain?"
I receive the same answer I would have been given
Had I asked, "Why me
To feel joy and sunshine?"
But then I did not ask.

And though I'm here now
In the hellish torment of loss,
I would not lose it.
I only know how high are the peaks
By the depths of the valleys.

Having walked in both shadow and sunshine,
In the blackness of night and the light of day,
I would not choose perpetual dusk
For its grayness would enter my soul.

I am both life and death,
Joy and sorrow,
Because I have lived both.

Because I have needed
and been given,
I can both give and receive.

In its proper time, I can be.

The first worst day
Was the day you died.
The second was burying you.
Then there was the day
You should have been
A month old, then two months.
Thanksgiving will come;
For what will I give thanks?
I'd intended to give thanks for your life.
Will I still be able to
Without damning him
For its shortness?
For I am thankful for every minute we shared.
Then there's Christmas
When his son was born -
And his son died.
Does that mean he knows my hell?
Then needing to believe
That as his son was resurrected,
Yet you have life and shall never die.
And if by chance
I survive Mother's and Father's Day,
Every year there'll be
The day you were born,
And then the days of another child
Who will ask me about you.
Someday, will there be
The last worst day?

I Am a Mother

I am a mother -
Sort of.
I have a son -
Somewhere.
I have two arms
To hold him
But they are empty.
I have a heart
That remembers him
And aches with love.

I gave birth to a life that died.
I have a son -
Somewhere.

I am his mother.

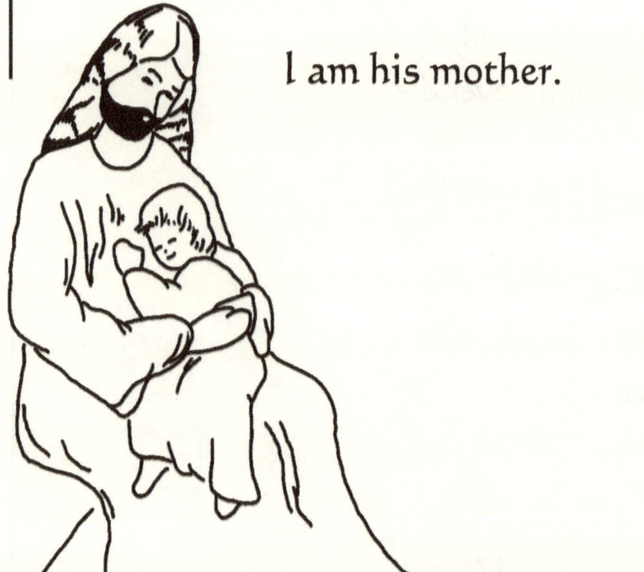

I am here where everything is the same;
I talk the same, I move the same -
So why is nothing the same?

Sometimes It's Not Enough

Sometimes sharing the pain is enough.
Sometimes being held is enough.
Sometimes the days and the nights are okay.

But how do you live through the hell
When the words make the pain more real,
And being held makes the loneliness more intense?

What do you do
When everything that is left
Is not enough?

Jehovah is my shepherd; I shall not want.
He maketh me to lie down in green pastures;
He leadeth me beside still waters.
He restoreth my soul:
He guideth me in the paths of righteousness
for his name's sake.
Yea, though I walk
through the valley of the shadow of death,
I will fear no evil; for thou art with me;
Thy rod and thy staff, they comfort me.
Thou preparest a table before me
in the presence of mine enemies:
Thou hast anointed my head with oil;
My cup runneth over.
Surely goodness and lovingkindness
shall follow me all the days of my life;
And I shall dwell in the house of Jehovah for ever.

Psalm 23

Grieving

Carry Me, Jesus

Carry me, Jesus, I pray.
My physical strength has deserted me.
My thoughts are in turmoil.
You alone are my hope.

Keep me, my Lord, with you
For without you, though I have the world,
I am totally alone.
You always are my friend.

Guide me, my God, through life.
Though I do not always understand my journey
And my feet falter on your path,
You, I know, will guide me home.

Grief

Yesterday
 You asked me
  If I was all right
  And I was.
   So today
    You do not understand
    Why,
     If the world was okay
      Yesterday,
       I fell into hell
       Today.

      Sometimes
       I think
        It would be easier
        To stand
         On the bottom
          Than to keep falling
          From the top.

           It's the crash that hurts.

I will not grieve forever
But right now I do need time.
Don't be hurt if I'm preoccupied,
If I can't be as strong or as steady
As you would wish.

I will not always be down
But don't make me lie or cover it.
Don't expect yesterday's smile to last forever.
There are many tears I've yet to cry;
Let me cry them.

And if I am able to laugh,
Do not tell me I did not love.
My grief is not over, nor my love forgotten.
If I am able to see my blessings,
Let me know joy.

Neither sorrow nor joy
Can hold their intensity forever.
There are ups in life and there are downs.
If we deny them, they are only delayed.
Let me feel them.

Who Are We Unshared?

I cannot handle your grief
Because I cannot see it,
I cannot feel it.
I am isolated from you.
I feel that at a time when we most need each other,
Our differences separate us.
I cannot share my grief
Because you cannot understand
That it is no less personal to me
Just because it is vocal.
Sometimes I feel the need to scream
    Or I will burst.
      How can you not explode
        When you cannot tell me how you feel?
        I don't mind leaving you some spaces
          Which you cannot share
          But how can I know you
          When you will share nothing?
          Everything I perceive and am
          Is coloured by my grief.
          Because we do not share this,
          We know nothing
            of each other.
            So who are we?

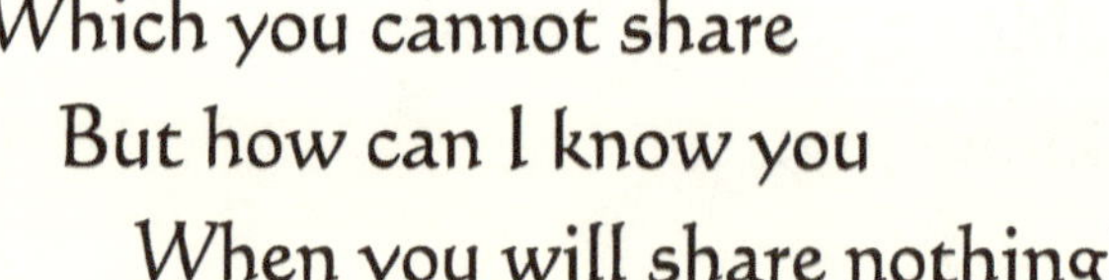

I depend on you, today, tomorrow.
You let me lean
        because my thoughts are too muddled
To show me that I still can stand.
I have time for very little but the pain.
I need you to have a little time for me;
To help me feel
        I have more substance than the hurt.

When I feel I'm smashed
        into a thousand scattered pieces,
Allow me the luxury
        of knowing you will pick me up,
And help put me together
So that someday you can look at me
And see me in one piece, standing alone,
Being more than I've ever been.

Blessed be the God and Father
of our Lord Jesus Christ,
the Father of mercies and God of all comfort;
who comforteth us in all our affliction,
that we may be able to comfort them
that are in any affliction,
through the comfort wherewith we ourselves
are comforted of God.

2 Corinthians 1:3-4

Living

We Are in This Together

We are in this together.
He was our son,
He was our joy
And our hope.
His death was our pain.
We are in this together.

We are in this apart
Because we are not the same.
Our feelings are separate,
Our love unique.
Our pain is handled in different ways.
We are in this apart.

We are in this with love.
With love we try to understand.
We reach out beyond our differences
So that though we pull in different ways,
We pull in the same direction.
We are in this together.

Guilt

I feel guilty
For not giving you a better chance,
For having a body that rejected you,
For being too ill to see you and be with you
For every moment you lived.

I feel guilty
Because I couldn't help you live,
Because I had no choice but to let you die,
Because I didn't have the words to tell you
How precious you really were.

I feel guilty
For being blessed with a beautiful child,
For receiving every wonderful thing you gave,
For having so little to give you in return
   For the gift of love.

      But I must remember
        I am not only guilty
           Of being frail and human and afraid.

      But also guilty
        Of loving more fully
             than I dreamed possible,
        Of giving as much of your life
             as it was possible to give,
        Of being able to receive your love
             and being blessed by it,
        Of doing all it was humanly
             possible for me to do.

         I am guilty
           And it is good.

God grant me my own forgiveness
As you have forgiven;
Grant me the strength to make today
A yesterday I won't regret,
And grant me the faith and the hope
And the trust in you.

Believing

I have written of the pain,
Of the memories,
Of the joy.
I have written of the fears,
Of the future,
Of the hope.
It will be many tomorrows
Before it hurts less.
It will always hurt some.
I believe I will be strong enough,
Through myself,
   Through my friends.
     I believe I will reach the day
       When the joy will be but lightly tinged
       With sorrow;
         When I will smile in remembering.
          I believe that
            not only will I survive,
           But I will survive well.

Thanks to all those
who encouraged me
in the writing,
who helped me in the living,
and who loved me.

June E. Shelly

And I saw a new heaven and a new earth:
for the first heaven and the first earth
are passed away; and the sea is no more.
And I saw the holy city, new Jerusalem,
coming down out of heaven from God,
made ready as a bride adorned for her husband.
And I heard a great voice out of the throne saying,
Behold the tabernacle of God is with men,
and he shall dwell with them,
and they shall be his peoples,
and God himself shall be with them,
and be their God:
and he shall wipe away every tear from their eyes;
and death shall be no more;
neither shall there be mourning,
nor crying, nor pain, any more:
the first things are passed away.
And he that sitteth on the throne said,
Behold, I make all things new. And he saith,
Write: for these words are faithful and true.
And he said unto me, They are come to pass.
I am the Alpha and the Omega,
the beginning and the end.
I will give unto him that is athirst
of the fountain of the water of life freely.

Revelation 21:1-6

Index

please note that first lines are written in italics

2 Corinthians 1:3-4   38
And I saw a new heaven and a new earth: 46
Believing   44
Blessed be the God and Father   38
Carry Me, Jesus   33
Carry me, Jesus, I pray.   33
Child Angel - illustration   32
Denial   17
The Difference   29
Feelings   13
The first worst day   27
For thou didst form my inward parts: 8
God Grant Me   43
God grant me my own forgiveness   43
Grief   34
Guilt   42
The Hurt, the Strength   21
I Am a Mother   28
I am a mother -   28
I am here where everything is the same;   29
I believe that tomorrow will come.   21
I cannot handle your grief   36
I Depend On You   37

I depend on you, today, tomorrow. 37

I feel guilty 42

I gave you the life you held so briefly, 12

I have written of the pain, 44

I know you are not there where last I saw you 17

I scream out, Why? 26

I will not grieve forever 35

In the beginning there was the seed 10

In the Incubator - illustration 16

It is said that some 18

Jehovah is my shepherd; I shall not want. 30

Let Me Feel 35

Letter of sympathy 9

A Loving Touch - illustration 40

Matthew 2:18 14

Matthew 19:13-14 22

Mother and Child - illustration 24

Mother to Son 12

My Son is Dead 19

My son is dead. 19

Our Love for James 10

Our son, James Thomas Shelly 9

Psalm 23 30

Psalm 139:13-14 8

Remembering 25

Revelation 21:1-6 46

Sometimes It's Not Enough   29

Sometimes sharing the pain is enough.   29

Thanks   45

Thanks to all those   45

Then were there brought unto him   22

Tomorrow Will Come   21

Too Young   18

A voice was heard in Ramah,   14

We Are in This Together   41

We are in this together.   41

We have so few pictures of you;   25

When I imagined the worst that could happen,   21

When I was pregnant, I was afraid;   13

Who Are We Unshared?   36

Why Me?   26

The Worst Day   27

Yesterday   34

Yesterday, there was a pregnancy.   20

Yesterday, Today, Tomorrow   20